Scottish Criminals

Scottish Criminals

Gary Smailes

Illustrated by Scoular Anderson

BIRLINN

For Margaret

First published in 2011 by
Birlinn Limited
West Newington House
10 Newington Road
Edinburgh
EH9 1QS

www.birlinn.co.uk

ISBN: 978 1 84158 931 2

British Library Cataloguing-in-Publication Data
A catalogue record for this book is available from the British Library

Typeset by Iolaire Typesetting, Newtonmore
Printed and bound by Grafica Veneta S.P.A., Italy

Contents

Introduction

We all know Scotland has produced loads of famous and brilliant people. We have all heard the stories of the super-Scots doing amazing deeds, ruling countries and generally being awesome. But, let's face it, are these the guys and gals that we really want to read about?

The problem is that their stories are often . . . well . . . boring.

So enter *Scottish Criminals*. This book brings you the little guys, the ordinary people who got caught up in history. They aren't kings and queens, they are simply scumbags and baddies. They are normal people (sort of!) who have just one thing in common: they have done something horrible that has left a little scratch in history. Some of the people you will meet in this book are pretty well-known and you may have come across them before, but the stories told here will shine a new light on their exploits (did you know William Wallace was a serial killer?). Others were troublemakers in their time but have since been forgotten . . . until now.

So forget the big guys, open the pages of this book and learn a little bit more about the normal people who have robbed, murdered and swindled their way into Scottish history.

1

Pirates

'Arghhh, Jim Lad. Pass me ma pieces of eight, whilst I get this landlubber to walk the plank.'

See, that's real pirate talk that is.

We all know that pirates are cute and cuddly, just misunderstood heroes after a pretty girl, a good time and some shiny gold. We've all seen the films – being a pirate is nothing but a bit of honest fun and swashbuckling adventure. Scottish pirates wouldn't really hurt anyone, would they?

Captain Kidd: Good Pirate or Bad Pirate?

Let's start our journey with one pirate who would like you to think he was, well . . . misunderstood. You know, a pussy cat that got caught up with a bad crowd. Here are some selected 'facts' about the life and times of Scottish pirate William Kidd.

William Kidd was born in Greenock somewhere around 1645. His early life is a bit of a mystery, though he is thought to be descended from Cornish gold-miners and we think his dad was probably a minister. What is certain is that at some point his father died and Kidd moved away from Scotland to live in New York, America.

By 1689 Kidd was all grown up and had taken to a life on the waves. He probably learned his trade by sailing with a number of small ships, some of them almost certainly pirate ships. However, it is possible that Kidd was just along for the ride and was never actually that bad. Below is a list of some evidence you can use to decide if Kidd was the notorious pirate that history would like us to believe.

Fighting for king and country

In 1689 Kidd was a member of a crew that mutinied (that's when the ship's crew captures the captain and takes over the ship). They renamed their ship *Blessed William*. Kidd became captain and used the ship to help protect the British Caribbean island of Nevis from being attacked by French ships. Because Kidd and his crew were not paid for their services, they decided to attack the French Caribbean island of Mariegalante, taking as much money and valuables as they could carry.

The king said it was ok

In 1695 Kidd was asked by the governors of New York, Massachusetts and New Hampshire to help attack and capture some pretty scary pirates who had been making a nuisance of themselves. Kidd needed a ship and crew, which all cost money. The money to pay Kidd came from a group of wealthy English noblemen. He was even given a letter from William III, King of England, giving him permission to attack pirates.

The moon's out

Captain Kidd had to go back to England to collect his new ship. It was called the *Adventure Galley*. It was brand new and turned out to be a bit leaky. He picked it up from Greenwich, but whilst sailing along the Thames he passed a British navy yacht. Kidd and his crew should have saluted but they didn't. The yacht's captain was pretty miffed and ordered a single cannonball to be fired towards the *Adventure Galley*. The response from Kidd and his crew was to line up along the side of their boat, expose their bare bum cheeks and slap them as they sailed past!

Worst pirate hunter – ever!

Kidd had been given a ship and a hat full of money to do one job – capture pirates. It turns out that Kidd was not the best pirate hunter in the world. Kidd sailed to a number of areas known to be places where pirates hung out, but he was unable to capture a single bad guy. By 1696 Kidd had spent months at sea without any success, and was getting desperate. He had attacked a convoy of pilgrims travelling to Mecca in the Middle East, but was beaten off and had to turn and run. He did spot a couple of well-known pirate ships, one from Holland, the other from America. However, by the time he had got his act together and prepared for an attack, the pirates had sailed off into the sunset. When Kidd and his crew finally returned to land, in 1697, many of his crew mutinied and ran off (perhaps out of embarrassment).

No more Mr Nice Guy

In the winter of 1697 Captain Kidd was once again at sea looking for pirates. They stumbled upon a known Dutch pirate ship but Kidd was reluctant to get involved. Kidd's gunner, William Moore, urged him to attack. Kidd refused, calling Moore a 'lousy dog'.

Moore replied, 'If I am a lousy dog, you have made me so; you have brought me to ruin and many more.' In a rage, Kidd smashed the side of Moore's head with a heavy bucket. Moore died the next day. The pirate got away – again.

From bad to worse

This was not the only act of violence related to Kidd. It is said that when prisoners tried to escape his ship he would have them hoisted up by the arms and beaten with the flat edge of a cutlass.

Now, where shall we begin?

It all goes wrong

In January 1698 Kidd came across a ship flying a French flag. He immediately attacked and captured the ship – a great prize. At first it seemed that Kidd had caught a vicious pirate. However, luck was not on Captain Kidd's side. It turned out that the captain of the pirate ship was English, and probably not even a pirate. Kidd knew that his masters back in England would not be happy and he urged his crew to let the ship go. They were having none of it –

they had sailed for months with no reward and had now captured a nice, big, juicy ship. They weren't going to give it up. Kidd had no choice but to keep the ship. When news spread to England that Kidd had captured an English captain, he was labelled a pirate and a price put on his head.

Kidd returned to America. He hoped that the important people who had paid for his voyage and new ship would help him out of the trouble he had found himself in – he was wrong! As soon as he set foot on dry land, he was arrested and thrown into prison. The conditions in prison were so bad, they sent poor Captain Kidd mad.

Mad Captain Kidd was sent to England for trial, where he was found guilty of murder and piracy and sentenced to death. They tried to hang Kidd, but the rope broke! He was hanged again, this time successfully. His body was then placed in an iron cage on the bank of the river Thames and left to rot.

Before we leave Captain Kidd, I must tell you about his buried treasure . . .

It has long been known that Kidd was very partial to burying his treasure. We know for sure that he buried a small chest of treasure at Gardiner's Island, off the east coast of America, because it was quickly found by a local gentleman.

However, there are still rumours that more, even bigger, chests of treasure remain buried to this day. The problem is that no one knows where! In 1983, two men were arrested and put in prison for nearly a year after they were found illegally entering the Vietnamese island of Phú Quốc. They said they were looking for Kidd's buried treasure.

There is also thought to be a huge chest of treasure buried on Clarke's Island, which lies in the Connecticut River at Northfield, Massachusetts. The story is that Kidd and his men sailed along the river to find a secret spot to bury their loot. After digging a hole and dropping the chest in, one of the pirates was murdered and his body was thrown into the hole too. Legend says that anyone finding the chest can only dig it up at midnight, when a full moon is overhead. Even then it can only be recovered by three men digging in silence . . .

The Sad Case of Captain Green

It seems that the English authorities were all too ready to hang poor Captain Kidd. But was it just the English who treated pirates harshly, or did the Scots also like to hang 'em high?

Our story starts around about the same time as Captain Kidd was searching the oceans for pirates. Thomas Green was the captain of a ship named the *Worcester*. One stormy night, the *Worcester* was forced to dock in the Firth of Forth. The local lawman, Roderick Mackenzie, wasted no time in arresting Captain Green and his crew, accusing them of boarding a ship called *Speedy Return*, killing the crew and stealing the cargo. This had all apparently taken place months before in the Indian Ocean.

Mackenzie had no evidence, but he was convinced that Green was a pirate and was not going to let such a small matter as having no evidence or witnesses saying Green had done nothing wrong, get in the way of a good *dis*honest trial. To make sure no one said anything to help Green, Mackenzie prevented all of Green's crew from giving evidence.

Green and his crew were found guilty and sentenced to be hanged.

When Mackenzie heard that the survivors of the *Speedy Return* were on their way back to Scotland, he made sure there were no delays in hanging Green. On 11 April 1705, a crowd gathered on Leith Sands to watch Green and two of his crew members, an Englishman, Simpson, and a Scot, John Madder, hanged to death. The three men were quiet in their final moments. Despite also being found guilty, the remaining members of the crew were released in the weeks following, after it became clear that they were probably not guilty after all.

Today, all the evidence suggests that Captain Green was NOT a pirate.

John Gow: Bad to the Bone

The reputation of pirates as bloodthirsty murderers and all-round bad guys is mostly well deserved. Though some Scottish pirates, like Captain Kidd, may have been lily-livered landlubbers, John Gow was bad to the bone.

John Gow was born in the Caithness town of Wick, around 1698, but he grew up in the town of Stromness in the Orkney Islands. Gow is pretty invisible to history until about twenty years later when he turns up in Amsterdam. There he joins a ship called *Caroline* as second mate and gunner.

Any problems, lads, just come to me!

Right from the start it is clear that Gow was a stirrer and troublemaker. The *Caroline* had its problems long before Gow stepped on board. The crew were unhappy with the food and the living conditions were really bad. The problem is that Gow made it worse, much worse. He joined in with the complaints and egged on the crew with talk of mutiny. The captain became worried and hid a pistol and ammunition in his cabin just in case he needed to protect himself.

We all have to start somewhere and 3 November 1724 was the day Gow became a pirate. It was a day that would go down in history. As the ship slept, Gow gathered a group of crewmen and crept silently through the cabins. Without making any noise, he sliced open the throats of the first mate, the ship's doctor and the supernumerary (the guy who was in charge of giving out pay) as they slept. Gow then headed towards the captain's quarters but was met by a storm of action. Arriving on deck, Gow discovered the wounded captain bravely fighting off three crew members. Gow pulled out a pistol and shot the captain twice in the stomach. As the captain collapsed, Gow jumped forward and stabbed him in the neck. Gow and his men threw the captain overboard. Amazingly, the captain was still alive and he managed to grab hold of a rope that dangled over the side of the ship. Gow calmly leaned over and sliced the rope, sending the captain to his death.

16

It turns out that even though Gow was as low as a snake's belly, he was not very bright. He had captured the ship but wasn't sure what to do next. In the end he decided to return home to the Orkney Islands, and pretend that he was now a wealthy merchant. Arriving at Stromness, all was well for the first few days, but it didn't take long for his old friends to become suspicious. Within a few weeks, the

truth was out. The townspeople turned on Gow and most of his crew ran away, leaving the wannabe pirate to fend for himself.

Gow fled Stromness and headed along the island coast. He was eager for more blood and more booty. Putting his ship at anchor, Gow headed inland to rob an expensive house he remembered from his childhood. Not happy with causing terror to its residents and stealing all the valuables he could find, he also kidnapped two servant girls.

In the end, it was Gow's stupidity that was his downfall. He could have sailed out to sea never to be seen again, but he was greedy for more easy booty. Greed and stupidity are never a good combination. Gow ordered his men once again to drop anchor so he could rob another house. But the ship ventured too close to the shore and became stuck on sand banks. Unable to escape, Gow was soon captured.

He was taken to England to face trial where our less-than-intelligent pirate once again proved he wasn't the sharpest cutlass in the box. You see, at the time it was possible to avoid a trial by refusing to plead. Pleading is saying that you are either guilty or innocent. If you kept your mouth shut and said nothing, there couldn't be a trial. This was Gow's plan. He would refuse to plead.

What he had forgotten was that the authorities were allowed to use torture to force a criminal to plead. At first Gow's thumbs were bound with a strong piece of string.

This stopped the blood and must have been very painful. But Gow still refused to talk. Unfortunately for our pirate, the authorities were just getting started. They calmly sat Gow down and explained what they would do to him if he refused to plead. They explained that they would lay him on the floor. They would then secure his two arms and two legs. Next, they would find as many heavy boulders and chunks of iron as they could. Then, one at a time, they would place the rocks and iron onto Gow's chest. They would keep piling them up until he either pleaded or died. They didn't really care which!

It was at this point that Gow finally opened his mouth . . . and claimed he was innocent! He said that he was not a pirate and it was all a huge misunderstanding.

The trial didn't take long and Gow was found guilty of murder and sentenced to death. A vicious pirate like Gow deserved a vicious death and that is just what he got.

In the moments before Gow was to be hanged, he asked the executioner to 'make it quick'. This meant that once Gow was hanging from the rope, the executioner would grab his legs and swing on them to break Gow's neck and speed up his death. So once Gow was hanging and jerking at the end of the rope, the executioner rushed down the ladder and heaved on the pirate's legs. Rather than Gow's neck breaking, it was the rope that snapped, sending the pirate and executioner to the floor in a huge heap. Gow lifted himself off the floor, walked back up the ladder and waited for a second rope.

This time he died quickly, swinging in the breeze. Gow's final humiliation came when his body was left to rot on the banks of the River Thames.

Do I have to do everything myself?

Alexander Dalzeel: Lucky and Clever

Not all Scottish pirates were stupid, greedy and blood-thirsty. Alexander Dalzeel was something far more frightening than a stupid, greedy and bloodthirsty pirate – he was a clever, greedy and bloodthirsty pirate.

Dalzeel was born in Port Patrick in Scotland around 1660. By the age of 23 he was the captain of his own ship, with a reputation as a lying, cheating scumbag. Dalzeel joined a fellow pirate by the name of Captain Avery and got caught up in a number of blood-soaked pirate adventures. But I am sure you have heard tales of ship boarding, princess kidnapping and gold burying before. What I want to show you here is that Dalzeel was one smart cookie.

Our pirate hero eventually parted company with Captain Avery and set out on his own. Yet in the months that followed he was unable to capture any ships, leaving his crew poor and desperate.

So, when a Spanish galleon appeared on the horizon, they didn't think twice before setting off to capture it. As Dalzeel edged nearer, they realised that the Spanish vessel was huge – far bigger than their weedy little ship. In fact, the captain of the Spanish ship took one look at Dalzeel's pirate ship approaching, skull and crossbones flying high, and went back to his cabin to play cards.

He won't bother us – he's a tiddler!

Let's get this in perspective. Dalzeel's ship was teeny tiny and the Spanish ship was super-big . . . surely Dalzeel was set for disaster. But remember, this guy was not John Gow. He had a big brain throbbing underneath his three-pointed pirate hat.

Dalzeel decided that the only chance they had of beating the Spanish ship was to give his crew no option but to win. So he ordered that a hole be made in the hull of his own ship. That's right, the crew were told to take a drill and make a hole between the nice dry inside of the ship and the rather wet and salty sea outside. Of course, the ship

flooded. Dalzeel's crew was left with two options: either they captured the Spanish ship or ended up in Davy Jones' Locker. Needless to say, with the added prospect of being shark food, Dalzeel and his men won the day, forcing their way onto the Spanish ship, capturing it in the process.

So is that it? Is that the one spark of Dalzeel's genius?

Not at all . . . here are some other schemes that got him out of a tight spot or two:

- Shortly after capturing the Spanish ship, Dalzeel was captured by a fleet of twelve Spanish ships. He should have been hanged or at least sold into slavery, but Dalzeel managed to sweet-talk his way out of trouble, convincing his enemy to let him go at the first bit of land they found.
- After being captured for a second time by the Spanish, Dalzeel was sentenced to be hanged at sea. However, he was able to escape once again. This time he stabbed

his captors and floated ashore using two empty jugs as floats.

- Once ashore, Dalzeel was able to convince another band of pirates not only to take him on as their leader, but also to attack the ship from which he had just escaped. The attack was a success. In the days following, the ship Dalzeel was sailing on was caught up in a storm and began to sink. This time he managed to jump into a small canoe and row himself to safety.
- After a number of successful and bloody years as a pirate, Dalzeel was once again captured – this time by the British. He was taken to England and sentenced to death. However, he was able to escape death again after the wealthy Earl of Mar convinced the king to let Dalzeel go free. The earl was an old mate of Dalzeel's, and he was also a bit of a bad guy.

- Our pirate hero was soon up to his old tricks and captured a French ship just off the coast of England. To amuse himself he had the crew tied up and thrown overboard. He stood and watched from the deck as they drowned.

Dalzeel's luck finally ran out in 1715 when he was arrested in Scotland. He was sent to London where he was once again sentenced to death. It was one capture too many and Dalzeel died at the hands of the hangman.

The Pirate's Code

You might think that pirating was all bloody chaos – stealing ships, fighting captains and getting hanged. But you would be wrong. Most pirate ships had their own rules, often written down, which told them what they were and weren't allowed to do. A bit like school rules but with swords.

Every pirate had to swear an oath to the code before he was allowed to join the pirate gang. Some would swear on the Bible, but they could also swear on a sword, an axe, crossed pistols or even a human skull. Some more theatrical pirates would swear their oath whilst sitting on a cannon.

Here are a few examples of rules from the Pirate's Code:

- Every pirate was entitled to have a share of all treasure and valuables captured.
- If a pirate was caught stealing from another pirate he would have his nose and ears sliced and then be put ashore at a remote place with 'one Bottle of Powder, one Bottle of Water, one small Arm [in other words a gun], and Shot [ammunition]'.
- Pirates were not allowed to fight on their ship – if one pirate hit another, he would receive forty lashes of the whip on his bare back. If two pirates had an argument they couldn't resolve, it had to be dealt with on shore. They would fight a duel with a single shot from a pistol and then fight with cutlasses until blood was drawn.

- All swords and pistols had to be kept clean and in working order.
- All lights and candles had to be out by eight o'clock.
- Musicians were not allowed to play on a Sunday.

These rules would be written down and placed on the door of the captain's cabin for all to see.

2

Assassins and Murderers

Some Scottish criminals are far more disturbing than 'cuddly' pirates with their eye patches and parrots. Some Scottish criminals are made of the stuff that will give you nightmares. What we have next is a collection of assassins and murderers whose names will be remembered for their foul deeds, bloodthirsty actions and pots of poison.

William Wallace:
Really Such a Good Boy?

We start our look at vicious assassins and murderers with one of the most famous Scots of all time – William Wallace. Some historians would like you to think Wallace was a hero, freedom fighter and all round good guy. However, the reality is very different and a lot more bloody.

The story of William Wallace begins around 1297. The English king, Edward I, had a plan to unite the British Isles and, having recently conquered Wales, Scotland was next on his list. However, Edward was busy in France and instead sent an army north to do his dirty work. The Scots were ready for them. Just outside the Scottish town of Stirling at a place called Stirling Bridge, two men, Andrew Moray and William Wallace, led the Scottish army into battle. The English army was defeated, but Moray was injured and later died.

Lots of historians would like you to believe that William Wallace was the brains behind the defeat of the English

army, but it is more likely that Moray was the mastermind and Wallace was just helping out. Wallace had the chance to prove he was a great general a year later when the English army invaded for a second time. The two armies clashed at Falkirk. But it wasn't like Stirling Bridge. To be honest, Wallace was a little bit rubbish as a general and the English army won an easy victory.

William Wallace escaped the battle and went into hiding in the Scottish Highlands. Many Scottish nobles now realised that fighting the English was pointless, so instead they negotiated with them. When the English invaded and took over Scotland, many of the Scots kept their lands and positions of power. However, for Wallace the idea of an English ruler was just too much.

No one knows for sure what happened to Wallace over the next seven years. Some historians say he went to meet the King of France to ask him for help, others say that he went to Rome. It is even suggested that he attacked and captured a pirate ship singlehandedly. What is known is that Wallace proved to be a real thorn in the side of the

English army. Our hero took to coming out of hiding, killing English soldiers in the night, and then disappearing into the Highlands – a bit like a kilt-clad serial killer.

It all ended in 1305. William Wallace had become an embarrassment to some of the Scottish lords. They wanted to get along with the English, but every time things were going well, Wallace would appear and kill more English soldiers. In the end, Wallace was captured when John de Menteith, a Scottish knight loyal to King Edward I, turned Wallace over to English soldiers at Robroyston near Glasgow.

Wallace was taken to London and faced trial in Westminster Hall. He was accused and found guilty of treason against King Edward I. After the trial, Wallace was stripped naked and dragged through the streets of London to Smithfield. Here he was hanged, drawn and quartered. His head was dipped in tar and placed on a spike on London Bridge. The four parts of his body were sent to be displayed in Newcastle, Berwick, Stirling and Aberdeen.

James Hamilton of Bothwellhaugh:
One Man and a Gun

Killing on the battlefield, or fighting for your freedom, is one thing. But to plan a murder and carry it out just so you can get your own way, is far more terrible. Here's our first Scottish assassin and be warned, he's no William Wallace.

It's a cold winter's night in 1570 and James Hamilton is part of a plot to kill Regent Moray.

I bet you are wondering just who Regent Moray was and why he was getting himself assassinated on a cold January night. It's all a bit complicated, but I will keep it simple.

Regent Moray was the 1st Earl of Moray, whose real name was James Stewart. He was the son of King James V of Scotland. This was a very confusing time in Scottish history with no obvious king or queen and lots of fighting between Protestants and Catholics. Some Scottish people wanted Mary, Queen of Scots, to be queen, others didn't and were happy to see Regent Moray ruling the country. He was not a king but had many of a king's powers.

OK, back to that cold winter's night in 1570. James Hamilton was part of a group of Scots who felt Scotland would be a much better place if Regent Moray was, well, . . . dead. Moray had been tricked into leaving Edinburgh, and Hamilton's gang knew he would spend the night in Linlithgow. Hamilton waited for Moray in a house which was four doors away from where Moray was sleeping, armed with a gun that had been given to him by the Abbot of Arbroath. Now this was a well-planned attack. Hamilton had placed a mattress on the floor to hide the noise of his footsteps. He had also hung black curtains on the walls to make sure he cast no shadows that could be seen from outside.

James Hamilton waited all night, hiding on a small balcony. The next morning, Moray rode out on his horse, intending to return to Edinburgh. When Moray was just a few feet away, Hamilton sprang from his hiding place and shot Moray off his horse.

Our assassin jumped onto his waiting horse and raced away. Moray's men were close behind and Hamilton had to ride hard. He used his spurs and whip to make the horse go faster but he was chased into a field and had his path

blocked by a wide pond. Fearing capture, Hamilton raced at the pond, and at the final moment stabbed his horse in the buttocks with the point of his knife, sending the poor animal over the pond and away to safety.

Moray died from his wounds and Hamilton fled to France.

What happened to James Hamilton after that is unknown. It is thought he was involved in two more assassination plots, one against Admiral Coligny, a pesky French leader, and one against William, Prince of Orange (who wanted to be king of France and England). It is rumoured that Hamilton managed to return to Scotland in secret and that his body is buried in the churchyard at Monkton. This might be a lie.

The one bit of good news for poor old Regent Moray is that he went down in history as the first person ever to be assassinated by a gun (it's not really good news for him, but it's interesting to us!).

Jean Livingston: Don't Be Mean to Girls

It's not just monstrous men who are capable of murder, sometimes gruesome girls can be just as bad.

In the summer of 1600, Jean Livingston, her old nurse Janet Murdo and her servant Robert Weir met in Livingston's house in Edinburgh to plan a murder. Livingston was married to John Kincaid of Warriston. He was a cruel man who mistreated his wife, often beating her. Livingston wanted out of the marriage but divorce was out of the question. It turned out that Jean's old nurse, Janet Murdo, had the perfect solution – murder – but the two women knew they couldn't do it on their own and decided to ask someone else to help. Robert Weir, Jean's servant, was talked into doing the deed.

We've got a wee ... er, task for you, Robert.

That night John Kincaid was provided with a bottle of wine and was left to stumble to bed drunk. Weir hid himself in the house and waited until he heard the clocks chime for midnight. He then emerged from his hiding place and

sneaked into Kincaid's bedroom. The intended victim was sound asleep, so Weir grabbed him and dragged him out of bed. Kincaid woke in a drunken haze to find Weir towering over him. Wasting no time, Weir pounced on Kincaid. In the struggle that followed, Weir wrapped his hands around Kincaid's throat and squeezed the life out of his victim.

News soon reached the police of the murder, and officers arrived at the house next morning. The police arrested Jean Livingston and Janet Murdo, but Robert Weir was nowhere to be found. At the trial that followed, Livingston showed no sadness at her husband's death. Jean Livingston and Janet Murdo were sentenced to be strangled and burned at the stake.

In the days before the execution, Livingston started talking to a priest, saying how sad she was at what had happened. The judge felt sorry for her and changed her sentence from strangulation to beheading. She would have her head cut off by a guillotine instead (he felt sorry for her, but not that sorry!). The two women were executed a few days later.

This is not quite the end of the story. Four years after the trial, Robert Weir was arrested. He was quickly found guilty and also sentenced to death. This time the judge was a bit more flamboyant with this method. He ordered that Weir to be hanged, but first to be 'broken on the wheel'. This grisly method of torture was hardly used in Scotland. Weir was tied to a cartwheel and then beaten with a wooden plough blade until his bones were broken and smashed. And then he was hanged.

The moral of this story? Don't be mean to girls, it just gets you into trouble.

John Hamilton: Gambled with His Life

I don't want you to think that Scotland is packed full of cold-blooded killers, but here's another cold-blooded killer . . .

It is 1715 and John Hamilton wants to join the army.

At that time the only way to become an officer was to give the army money so that they would give you a job. Hamilton had convinced his rich parents to give him the cash and he had travelled to Edinburgh with the intention of signing up. But with the money burning a hole in his pocket, Hamilton instead joined a card game and lost the lot.

Stony-broke, Hamilton did the only thing he knew how to do – asked his parents for more money. Reluctantly they agreed and within a few days he was once again ready to sign up. I am sure he had every intention of signing up, but when he heard of a card game running at a pub just outside Glasgow he couldn't resist.

The game went on for two days and nights, with none of the gamblers taking a break. In the end Hamilton fell asleep at the table. When he woke he found his fellow gamblers had gone, and the pub owner, Thomas Arkle, was standing over him insisting that he pay their rather large bill.

Hamilton had lost all his money and didn't know what to do.

Being a coward, Hamilton decided to make a run for it. He sprang from his chair and made for the door. The landlord dived at Hamilton's legs, but missed and instead gripped the scabbard of John's sword. John got away but he decided he wanted his scabbard back. So, with sword in hand, he returned to the pub. The landlord was waiting. An argument ensued and in the chaos Hamilton stabbed Thomas Arkle in the chest.

Leaving his sword stuck in the dead innkeeper, Hamilton turned and ran. This time it was the dead landlord's daughter that tried to stop him. She grabbed at Hamilton but was left holding part of his coat, which had ripped as he made his getaway. The police were called and the sword and material were used as evidence against Hamilton.

Hamilton escaped to Holland and remained there for two years. However, when his parents died, he faced a problem. To collect his inheritance (the money his parents had left him in their will), he needed to go back to Scotland. Hamilton had no choice but to return. He sailed back to Scotland but was immediately recognised, arrested and found guilty of murder. On 30 June 1716, John Hamilton came face-to-face with the Scottish maiden (we aren't talking about a young lady here – the Scottish maiden was a type of guillotine!). A crowd had gathered in Edinburgh's Grassmarket for the occasion and a huge cheer erupted as our criminal hero's head was chopped clean from his body.

Daniel McNaughtan: A Madman

I suppose you could argue that most of the people in this book were mad in one way or another, but Daniel McNaughtan is the first bad guy we come across who was actually able to prove he was insane. He was born in Glasgow in 1813 and, after an unsettled childhood, he trained as a carpenter. He left Glasgow to become an actor, but after three years returned to Glasgow and set up business as a carpenter.

For the following five years all was going well for McNaughtan. His business grew, he saved money and was well liked. Then, at Christmas-time 1839, he suddenly sold his business and disappeared to London. Over the next few years he moved about the country, keeping in touch with his friends and family. Whenever they met up with him, McNaughtan seemed worried and scared. He complained that the government was out to get him and that he was being followed by spies.

It is not until 20 January 1843 that our villain once again re-appears in history. The day in question was cold with few people on the streets of London. It was later reported that McNaughtan was seen hanging around near the Houses of Parliament. Sometime in the afternoon, the

politician Edward Drummond started to walk from 10 Downing Street, where he had met with the prime minister, towards Charing Cross. McNaughtan ran up behind Drummond, pulled out a pistol and shot him in the back. Drummond slumped to the ground and McNaughtan was wrestled down by two policemen. McNaughtan later told the police that he thought he had shot the Prime Minister. At first it looked like Edward Drummond would survive, but after being treated by doctors (he received special treatments which included leeches sucking his blood), he died a few days later.

Having been caught red-handed, McNaughtan never denied shooting Drummond. However, when his case finally came to court, McNaughtan claimed that he was insane and was not in his 'right mind' at the time of the killing. Let's get this straight – McNaughtan claimed that because he was mad he was not guilty of murder. As you can guess, people were pretty angry. But the trial was fairly straightforward. A number of doctors and lecturers agreed that McNaughtan was indeed mad, and the jury were left with little choice but to find him not guilty.

So he walked away free? No. McNaughtan was in for a shock. Since he was now deemed insane, he was sent to the state criminal lunatic asylum at Bethlem Hospital. McNaughtan ended up spending 21 years in the asylum, before finally dying of diabetes.

Thomas Cream: A Killer Abroad

Some Scottish criminals are not satisfied with a quick sword stabbing or a shot from a gun. Some of the more creative murderers have to over-complicate the matter, spreading their killing across the globe.

Thomas Cream was a colourful character from the start and seemed destined for either fame or infamy – unfortunately for his victims he was never famous . . .

Our story begins in Glasgow in 1850. Thomas Cream was born a Scot but his family moved to Canada when he was young. His father was a shipbuilder and Cream trained in shipbuilding too and joined his father's business.

In 1872 it had become clear to Cream's dad that his son was no shipbuilder. So Cream was sent to Montreal to study as a doctor – this is when we start to get an indication that everything was not quite right with the young man. In one account he is described as 'rather wild and fond of ostentatious displays of clothing and jewellery'.

He became obsessed with a chemical called chloroform. This smelly chemical has the power to knock unconscious anyone who sniffed it.

This is not enough to single out a young doctor as a madman, but in 1876 Cream's flat burned to the ground. It was thought that he had set it alight himself, but nothing was ever proved.

Soon after the fire Cream married, but only weeks after the ceremony he set sail for London, leaving his wife behind. In London he finished his studies and became a doctor.

It was during this time that the next unusual event took place. Cream and his wife were still apart, but when his wife fell ill Cream sent medicine all the way from London to Canada. His wife took the medicine and died shortly afterwards. Once again Cream was suspected of a crime, but no evidence could be found to prove he had actually poisoned his unfortunate wife.

From 1879 to 1881 Thomas Cream was a doctor in London, Ontario; and Chicago. At least two of his patients died in suspicious circumstances but, as usual, nothing could be pinned on him.

The law finally caught up with our doctor in Belle Rivière, Ontario. Here he was arrested for the murder of a patient, Daniel Stott. He was found guilty on 23 September 1881 and sent to prison for life.

If this was the end of Cream's story, he would be just a run-of-the-mill murdering doctor. But he is a *Scottish Criminal* and so there's more . . .

In 1891, after just ten years in prison, Cream was released for good behaviour. His father died shortly afterwards (we don't think Cream had anything to do with this one, which makes a change!) and left Cream some money.

Cream went to London. Records of people who knew Cream at this time call him a 'foul-mouthed, frightening, drug addict' and 'lonely and restless, talking endlessly of women, money and poison'.

Soon after Cream moved to London, two women were killed close to his flat. Cream was never convicted of these murders but it seems very possible he was involved. Cream was now out of control. He had tasted blood and couldn't stop killing. Soon after the deaths of the first two women, two more were found dead and when Emma Shrivell and Alice Marsh were killed by poison, Cream became the prime suspect. He quickly shifted the blame to a young medical student called Harper.

The police in England looked into Cream's past in America and were able to arrest him for the murder of a woman called Matilda Clover. They soon added three other murders to the list and the attempted murder of yet another woman.

Thomas Cream was hanged at Newgate prison at 9 a.m. on 15 November 1892. More than 4,000 people turned up to watch him swing by his neck. After Cream was cut down, Madame Tussaud's, the waxwork museum, paid £200 for a set of his clothes. They dressed a waxwork model in the clothes and charged the public to see the display. Perhaps Cream was famous after all, or at least his clothes were!

DR. THOMAS CREAM

Black Widows of Liverpool

Scottish criminals are generous people and they often like to spread their crimes far beyond the borders of Scotland. As we saw from Dr Cream, this might be as far as Canada and America, but this rather nasty pair of sisters shows us that only a few hundred miles south is sometimes enough.

Not much is known about the early life of the two sisters who were called the Black Widows of Liverpool. We know they were born in Scotland and moved to Liverpool when young women.

It all began in 1881, when Thomas Higgins, his wife and his daughter went to live in the same house as Catherine Flanagan in Liverpool. Catherine Flanagan (we will call her Widow 1) owned the house and Thomas Higgins paid her rent.

Only a few months after Higgins moved in, his wife died in very suspicious circumstances indeed. Along came Margaret (who we will call Widow 2). She was the sister of Widow 1. She had been married before, but her husband had died in suspicious circumstances (see a pattern here?).

Widow 2 wasted no time and within a few months she had married Thomas Higgins.

The next victim was poor Mary, Thomas Higgins' daughter. She died in (yes, you've guessed it) suspicious circumstances shortly after the marriage.

Almost exactly one year after young Mary popped her clogs, Thomas Higgins himself was bumped off and it was a hat trick for the widows. It was all too much for Higgins' brother who insisted that the police look into his death. It turned out he had been poisoned by arsenic taken from flypaper. There was only one suspect – well, two actually!

The police now acted quickly and dug up the bodies of three other people who were connected to the widows. The first was Widow 1's son, who had died aged 22. The second was an 18-year-old lodger called Maggie Jennings. The third was young Mary Higgins. All three had been poisoned with arsenic.

On 3 March 1884 Widow 1 and Widow 2 were hanged side-by-side at Kirkdale Prison. They were convicted of four murders, but are thought to have killed as many as seventeen people!

Richard Archer Prince:
Acting Like a Killer

So far we have seen lots of murderers who were bad, but just one who was mad. So let's even the balance with another Scottish murderer, who lost his marbles,

Richard Archer Prince was born in Dundee and had always wanted to be an actor. He followed his dream and moved to London. By 1887 he was appearing on stage in a number of small parts. It was at this time that Prince met William Terriss, a famous actor. Terriss took a liking to Prince and helped him get parts in plays.

I think I can find you some work.

This might have been the end of our story, with Richard Archer Prince becoming a successful actor and living happily ever after . . . but that's not the kind of story we like to tell! It turns out that Prince was a bit of a drunk and, well, more than a little bit insane. By 1895 he was well known in London theatres, not as a great actor, but as 'Mad Archer'.

It all started to go wrong for Prince in 1897. He was acting in a play called *The Harbour Lights* with Terriss. The two men had an argument and Terriss had Prince sacked. Prince reacted badly. On 13 December he was thrown out

of the Vaudeville Theatre and the next night he was heard arguing with Terriss in his dressing room at the Adelphi Theatre. On 16 December, Prince was seen acting even more strangely than usual outside the Adelphi Theatre where Terriss was due to be on stage that night. When Terriss finally turned up, Prince jumped from the shadows and stabbed Terriss in the back, side and chest. He died from his wounds.

Prince was caught shortly afterwards and told the police, 'I did it for revenge. He had kept me out of employment for ten years, and I had either to die in the street or kill him.'

In the trial that followed it was claimed that Prince was insane, which was no surprise to anyone. In fact, Prince's mother and doctors were happy to stand in court and declare that Prince was as mad as a March hare. Prince was sent to Broadmoor Hospital, a criminal lunatic asylum, where he spent the rest of his life. Apparently Prince was the conductor of the hospital orchestra until his death.

Archibald Hall: A Man with a Plan

Some of the criminals in this book seem to be people who were just in the wrong place at the wrong time, others were driven to their crimes fighting for what they believed was right, others still were just born bad – like Archibald Hall.

Archibald Hall was stealing by the age of 15. He came from Glasgow but as a young man he moved to London to try and sell some stolen jewellery. He was caught and sentenced to a short spell in prison. Whilst in prison he came up with a plan – when he was released he would become a butler and then steal from the rich. He read books on etiquette which taught him about good manners and polite behaviour, and also took lessons to learn to speak with a posh accent.

In 1975 Archibald Hall, now a free man, returned to Scotland. He got a job as a butler for Margaret Hudson, who lived at Kirtleton House in Dumfriesshire. Hall had planned to steal from the old lady, but he grew to like her and settled down to a normal life. However, one morning a man called David Wright turned up at Kirtleton House. He was the new gamekeeper. Hall was upset at seeing Wright. They had met in prison some years before and Wright knew all about Hall's criminal past.

Hall knew he needed to get rid of Wright and lured Wright into a field, shot him dead and buried him next to a stream. Archibald Hall knew his chances of going straight had now disappeared, so he quit his job and returned to London.

Our hero soon returned to his original plan, to become a butler and rob the rich. He found a job working for 82-year-old Walter Scott-Elliot, and his 60-year-old wife Dorothy. Unfortunately for Hall, Dorothy Scott-Elliot walked in on him discussing his plan to kill and rob his employers with another man called Michael Kitto. Hall immediately grabbed the old lady and suffocated her. He then drugged Walter Scott-Elliot and drove him and his dead wife up to Scotland, stopping in a hotel on the way. He buried Dorothy in Braco, Perthshire, and then after strangling Walter buried him in woods near Tomich, Inverness-shire.

Hall and Kitto had asked a friend called Mary Coggles to help them get rid of the bodies. In return, they had given Coggles the dead woman's jewels and fur coat. Coggles took to wearing these around town and the murdering pair soon realised they had made a mistake. In the winter of 1977 Hall and Kitto killed Coggles and left her body in a barn in Middlebie, Dumfriesshire.

Our murdering butler had one last score to settle – with his half-brother. Hall had always hated him. Since his brother had just been released from prison, Hall decided the time was right for revenge. Hall and Kitto travelled to his half-brother's house in Cumbria. They used chloroform to knock Hall's half-brother out and then drowned him in a bath.

Hall and Kitto planned to travel to Scotland to bury the body (why he couldn't just bury it in England we will never know – maybe you have to be a psychopathic murderer to understand), but the roads were very icy and snow was falling hard. The pair were worried that if they crashed the car the police would find the dead body in the boot. In the end they decided to spend the night in a hotel and continue their journey the next morning. However, the owner of the hotel thought they were acting suspiciously and called the police, who didn't take long to find Hall's dead half-brother. Kitto was arrested but Hall escaped through a toilet window, only to be caught a few miles down the road.

In the end, Hall was convicted of four murders and spent the rest of his life in prison. He wrote his autobiography from his prison cell, which was published just before he died in 2002.

3

Outlaws

Let's be honest, we all love a good outlaw. The romance of the open road, the glamour of armed robbery and the excitement of eating raw human flesh!

Sorry, wait there . . . what am I saying?

Forget the romance and glamour – some of Scotland's scariest outlaws were horrible, stinking, violent men and women, who not only lived outside the law, but wouldn't think twice before popping you in an itchy bag and carrying you off to their secret lair to serve you up for dinner!

Sawney Bean: He Would Eat Your Face!

Travel north along the A77 from the Scottish town of Stranraer and you will eventually come to the sleepy village of Ballantrae. If you are brave, keep heading north until you come to Bennane Head, an outcrop of land which thrusts into the sea. If you stand at the edge of the car park and peer down over the cliff, 150 feet below you will see the narrow opening to a cave. This was once the home of a tribe of cannibals who killed more than 1,000 people!

Local legend tells us that Alexander Bean was born in East Lothian in the sixteenth century. He was a vicious and lazy man, and he ran away with a local woman who was equally as mean. They made a home in the deep, damp cave at Bennane Head and set about raising a family. They lived in the cave undetected for 25 years as their clan grew to 18 members.

Oh, what a lovely home!

Sawney (as he became known – 'Sawney' was an English nickname for a Scotsman) had a big family to provide for. He didn't want a job and certainly had no intention of wearing a tie (unless it was made of human skin, then I suspect he may have made an exception). So he took to sneaking out at night and robbing and killing local people as they travelled along the nearby roads. Sawney didn't like spending money on unnecessary items such as . . . say . . . food. So he would take the bodies of his victims back to his cave, cut them up and eat them for tea. The bits his family didn't eat were pickled and saved for later!

As the years went by, and more and more people vanished, locals became certain that something evil was lurking close by. This is where King James VI of Scotland joins the story. King James was a bit mad and was obsessed with the idea that people were trying to kill him. At one point he became so convinced that witches were planning his death that he set up hundreds of trials, burning loads of innocent women (who he thought were witches) at the stake. Well, it turns out he was pretty petrified of cannibals too. So when he heard of the disappearances, he organised a party of 400 men to hunt down the clan. It didn't take them long to find the cave and capture the cannibals.

The whole Bean clan was sentenced to execution. The men had their private parts (ouch!), hands and feet cut off and were then left to bleed to death. The women and children were made to watch the men die before being burned alive!

Some historians will try to convince you that Sawney Bean never existed, but they are just spoilsports who have clearly never heard the story of the Hairy Tree.

This legend says that Sawney Bean's eldest daughter escaped capture and travelled a few miles north to Girvan. Here she planted a tree. When the local villagers discovered Miss Bean's cannibal past they hung her from the tree until she was dead. Many believe the tree is still standing today and that if you stand quietly under its branches you can hear the sound of the swinging corpse.

Christie Cleek: A Real Cannibal

So, some historians think that Sawney Bean never existed. They might be right, but one Scottish cannibal that certainly (well, maybe) lived was Christie Cleek.

Andrew Christie was a butcher from Perth who lived even longer ago than Sawney Bean, way back in the fourteenth century. Times were tough in Scotland and food was not easy to find. A group set off into the Grampian foothills to try and find some nice grub. When one of the gang died in an unfortunate accident, Christie was quick to put his butchery skills to the test, whipping up a quick dish of human flesh.

Seems a pity to waste such prime meat!

Christie must have cooked a mean meal because the gang were sold on this new source of food. With Christie as their leader they took to ambushing passing travellers and eating them and their horses. Legend tells us that Christie would jump from his hiding place and pull the riders from their horses using a metal hook attached to a long pole, a weapon known locally as a cleek, hence the name Christie Cleek.

The gang was eventually captured, but it is rumoured that Christie Cleek escaped and returned to normal life . . . as a butcher!

Johnnie Armstrong: He Shouldn't Have Trusted the King

Not all outlaws enjoyed the taste of human flesh. Some just didn't get along with the rulers of their country.

The Scottish clans that lived in the borderlands between England and Scotland in the sixteenth century made it their duty to terrorise their English neighbours. And when it came to rubbing up the English the wrong way, Clan Armstrong were masters.

King James V of Scotland needed to prove that he was a strong leader and the biggest threat to his power was the clan leaders who lived in the Scottish Borders. James decided that these clan leaders must be defeated once and for all, so in 1530 he gathered an army of 8,000 men and marched south.

We're going to the Borders. Find me a small army.

Yes, sire.

The first victims of James' soldiers were Cockburn of Henderson and Scott of Tushielaw. These men were quickly captured and then first hanged outside the walls of their castles before being sent, half-dead, to Edinburgh.

Who was the next outlaw on James' hitlist? Johnnie Armstrong.

Johnnie Armstrong wasn't some casual hooligan, this guy was a serious badass. In fact, he was the undisputed king of the Borders and the number-one tormentor of Scottish kings and Englishmen alike.

Armstrong's favourite game was to cause trouble. He wasn't too fussy about where this trouble happened. Sometimes it would be in Scotland, sometimes he would cross the border into England. He and his men would steal cattle, rob farms, burn houses, in fact do just about anything they wanted.

By the time James' army marched into the borderlands Armstrong had gathered himself a sizable army of his own. He could muster 160 armed and angry Scottish warriors.

James knew that Armstrong would avoid a battle at all costs. After all why would a clan leader with just a couple of hundred Highlanders try to take on the huge, well-trained and well-armed army? So the king came up with a cunning plan. James summoned Armstrong and his men to come and meet him and go hunting together. Johnnie

knew that refusing to go to the king was an act of treason that would have meant the king's army hunting them down. So they went. Legend tells us that they met at Carlenrig. The outlaws were dressed in expensive and flashy clothes. An ancient song says that Armstrong wore 'a girdle embroidered and bespangled with gold and his hat with its nine targes each worth three hundred pounds'.

However, James had no intention of going hunting with the outlaws and had set a trap. When Armstrong and his men arrived, they were immediately arrested. At first Armstrong tried to talk his way out of trouble, but the king was having none of it. Next, he tried bribery, and when that didn't work he simply insulted the king. What did the king do? Did he have a change of heart, give all the men detention and send them home after a stern telling-off?

No . . .

James took Armstrong and 36 of his men to the local chapel and hanged them from the trees. This sent out a very clear message – mess with King James V and you'll end up dead!

One of the reasons we know so much about what happened to Johnnie Armstrong is because a very famous song was written about the outlaw and his exploits. It was called 'The Ballad of Johnnie Armstrong of Gilnockie' (catchy title, eh?).

But Armstrong was not the only outlaw whose story is remembered in a song . . .

Jamie MacPherson: Captured by a Blanket

Jamie MacPherson may have been forgotten by history if he had not written down his life in the form of a song. But we are jumping the gun a bit. Let's first take a look at MacPherson and see what he has done that is worthy of a song. I don't think I am spoiling the surprise when I say MacPherson wasn't a good guy. He lived about 150 years after King James V had hanged Johnnie Armstrong from that tree outside Carlenrig chapel.

Our outlaw hero was the son of a Scottish Highland laird and a beautiful gypsy girl. When MacPherson was only a child his father was killed by outlaws trying to steal his father's cattle and he was brought up by his mother. MacPherson and his mother were looked after by the local gypsy tribes – they were given money and were always well dressed. As MacPherson grew into a man he became a great sword-fighter and was renowned for his fiddle-playing. It was not long before he was leading the band of gypsies that had provided for him when he was child.

We now get to a part in the story that seems to me a bit too good to be true. Many of the accounts of Jamie MacPherson say that he was a great bloke who loved his granny, stroked kittens and helped old ladies across the road. Oh yeah, and he was also the leader of a cut-throat band of robber gypsies.

Jamie MacPherson's gang was a bunch of lowlife thieves. They carried out a string of robberies in Aberdeenshire. It appears that MacPherson was caught at least three times, each time either escaping or being rescued. In 1700 he was captured a fourth time and was due to face trial when the Laird of Grant, an old mate of MacPherson's, stepped in to save him from certain death.

Now under the protection of the laird, MacPherson and his men went wild. His band of gypsies took to marching into local markets with a piper at the head of the gang. They would then rob and steal from the crowd. This happened at markets in Banff, Elgin and Forres.

Then MacPherson's luck changed. The Laird of Grant was arrested for carrying a weapon and was hanged at Banff. It was decided that MacPherson would be next. He was cornered at St Rufus Fair at Keith in Moray. A massive fight broke out and one of MacPherson's men was killed. MacPherson was finally captured when a woman dropped a blanket onto his head from a window of a house.

MacPherson was sentenced to be hanged and it was while in prison that the outlaw wrote his famous song – he called it 'MacPherson's Lament' but it became known as 'MacPherson's Rant'.

What happened in the final moments of MacPherson's life is once again open to some debate. I will give you the version I think MacPherson would have liked you to hear.

On the day of his death, MacPherson walked calmly to the gallows. His final wish was to sing his song. He was given his fiddle and proceeded to sing 'MacPherson's Rant'. Once the song was over he took the fiddle and smashed it over the executioner's head and threw it into the crowd. MacPherson was then hanged. The fiddle survived (unlike MacPherson) and can be found, broken, in the MacPherson Clan museum near Newtonmore, Inverness-shire.

One legend that surrounds MacPherson's hanging is rather interesting. It seems that MacPherson was due to be hanged on the hour. When the local sheriff heard news that a letter was being brought from the local lord which instructed MacPherson to be set free, the sheriff decided to take action. The legend says he moved the clock forward by 15 minutes, allowing the hanging to go ahead. Even to this day it is reported that the town of Macduff has one face of its town clock covered so the people of neighbouring Banff can't see the correct time!

Rob Roy: Hero or Villain?

One person's outlaw is another person's hero. Some out-laws are downright evildoers with nothing in mind except gold, fighting and maybe a few fancy girlfriends. But some-times an outlaw is a good guy, especially when he is fighting for what he thinks is right. Rob Roy was one such outlaw.

Let's clear something up before we start – Rob Roy had a few different names. His real name was Robert Roy Mac-Gregor. In Scotland he was known as Raibeart Ruadh, which means Red Robert – when he was a young man he had a shock of red hair, hence the name. Most common of all was Rob Roy, and that's what we will call him.

Rob Roy was born in Glengyle, at the head of Loch Katrine, sometime around 1671. Up until the age of 18, Rob Roy led a quiet life in the Scottish Highlands. But the battles of the famous Jacobite Risings changed his life forever.

It all started with James VII of Scotland and II of England. He was a Catholic. Lots of people in England didn't want a Catholic king. In 1688 James was forced off the throne and replaced by William III and James' daughter Mary II.

King James had lots of supporters – called 'Jacobites' – most of them in Scotland and Ireland. In 1689 a group of men in Scotland decided to form an army to try to put James back on the throne. Rob Roy's family joined in this fight, and so did Rob Roy. At first the fight went well but Rob Roy's father was soon arrested and thrown in prison. His mother became ill and died.

In 1719 Rob Roy fought against the English army in the Battle of Glen Shiel. The battle started when government soldiers moved into the area to defeat a band of rebels that contained not only Rob Roy, but also other Highlanders and even some Spanish troops. The rebels had set up a barricade across a main road and also dug trenches into a nearby hillside. It was in these defences that the rebels, with about 1,000 soldiers, waited for the English army. They finally showed up on 10 June 1719, with 850 soldiers on foot, 150 soldiers on horseback and 4 cannons. They came marching along the road, ready to do battle.

The rebels held firm at first, but as the battle wore on they were pushed out of their defences and forced to retreat.

Rob Roy was severely injured but survived the battle.

Aside from rising up against the English army, he had not really done anything to make him an outlaw. Lots of Highlanders joined the rebellion and lots fought against the English, but only a few became outlaws. Rob Roy's problems with the law began with cows!

Having got all the rebelling out of his system, Rob Roy settled down to raise cattle. It turned out he was a great cattle farmer. The problem Rob faced was that to make lots of money he needed lots of cows, and cows cost money. Rob didn't have much cash so he decided to borrow some money to buy cows.

When the time came to repay the loan, Rob claimed he couldn't. This is where the story gets a bit confusing. One version says that Rob had given his borrowed cash to his head cattle herder and sent him off to buy more cows. The herder never came back and it was the last Rob Roy saw of the cash. Another version says that Rob Roy himself stole the money and never had any intention of buying cows. Whatever the truth, the law got involved.

Rob Roy was declared an outlaw and it was all downhill from there. Rob owed the money to James Graham, 1st Duke of Montrose, who decided to take Rob's land in repayment. Rob's wife and his family were kicked out of their house, which was then burned to the ground. This left our man pretty peeved and Rob Roy declared a blood feud against the Duke of Montrose.

Rob Roy became a thorn in the side of the Duke of Montrose. He took to stealing from the duke's lands and even kidnapping one of the duke's men, holding him captive on an island in Loch Katrine.

In 1722 Rob Roy's luck ran out. We don't know the details of what happened, but what we do know is that by 1722 Rob Roy had been captured and was serving a five-year prison sentence.

This might have been the last we heard of Rob Roy but the famous writer Daniel Defoe (he wrote *Robinson Crusoe*) had other ideas. Defoe was fascinated by Rob Roy's story and was inspired to write a book called *Highland Rogue* all about the outlaw. Many people read the book and then put pressure on the king to order Rob Roy to be released. You see, the book made Rob Roy out to be a misunderstood hero, and we know all about misunderstood heroes! As with most of these stories, much of what Defoe wrote was not true. None of this mattered. In 1727 Rob Roy was just about to be sent away from the country on a prison ship, when the king issued a pardon and Rob Roy was set free.

Rob Roy returned to the Trossachs. He died in 1734 and was buried at the church at Balquhidder. A few years later, the bodies of Rob Roy's wife Mary and his sons Coll and Robin were buried next to his grave.

4

Thieves

We've had pirates, murderers and outlaws. Now it's time for some good old-fashioned robbers. This time I am not going to try and pull the wool over your eyes with mis-understood heroes, do-gooders and outlaws that were more in than out. This collection of lawbreakers will not let you down – they are all good-for-nothing, robbing Scottish scumbags (well, most of them).

William Brodie:
Good in the Day but Bad at Night

Once again we return to Edinburgh. This time it's 1768.
William Brodie is a respected cabinet-maker, head honcho
of his local group of carpenters and a big fish in the local
council. This gives him the nickname of Deacon Brodie.
He is an important man in Edinburgh, seen at all the right
parties, friends with all the important people and a good
guy to know . . .

Brodie's problem was that he got bored easily. His
important life and job as a cabinet-maker were . . . well,
. . . boring. Brodie would often go to the cockpit in

Edinburgh's Grassmarket to watch two cockerels fighting – he would place a bet on which cockerel he thought would be the victor. He enjoyed the excitement. He also enjoyed talking with the people he met there. These were not important people like him, they were criminals and thieves. It gave him an idea.

Brodie's job meant he was invited into some of the most expensive houses in Edinburgh. Not only did he make cabinets but was also an expert with locks. One fateful day in 1768, Brodie was invited to look at the locks of a nearby

bank. The temptation was too great. He made a wax impression of the keys to the bank and from this he was able to make his own copy of the keys. He returned to the bank the next night, crept inside and stole £800 (more than £100,000 in today's money).

The thrill of the crime was everything Brodie was looking for and he was hooked. From that day on, he led two lives. During the day he was a well-respected man about town, at night he was a thief and all-round bad guy. His plan was pretty simple. When he was invited to look at the locks of a well-to-do family's house, he would make a wax impression, copy the keys and go back and rob the house. His scheme was so successful that within a few months he had recruited a gang of three other crooks.

Brodie's career as a thief didn't last long and came to a sudden end. Brodie had become increasingly brave and conjured up a plan to raid a tax office on the Canongate. Things didn't go Brodie's way. One of his gang was captured and he told the police all about the others. Brodie was forced to flee and set sail for Holland, hoping to make it to America. The police caught up with him in Amsterdam, where he was arrested and shipped back to Edinburgh for trial.

When the police searched Brodie's house, they found copied keys from houses that had been robbed, a disguise and a set of pistols. The trial began on 27 August 1788. It didn't take long for the jury to find him guilty. Brodie was hanged at the Tolbooth on 1 October 1788. What must have been most annoying for Brodie was that the wooden gallows on which he was hanged had been designed and even paid for by him some years earlier!

But the twists and turns of Brodie's life story don't end there.

There is a rumour that Brodie tried to escape death. He had a metal ring made and inserted into his shirt collar. He also placed a silver tube down his throat. His plan was to let the executioner hang him but then be taken away and revived afterwards. His plan failed and he was buried at Buccleuch Parish Church.

The writer Robert Louis Stevenson, who lived in Edinburgh, became obsessed with William Brodie's story. Stevenson's father even owned furniture that was made by Brodie. Robert Louis Stevenson's tribute to our first thief came in the form of the book *The Strange Case of Dr Jekyll and Mr Hyde*. In this famous story, a respectable man about town drinks a potion that makes him a monster at night.

John Reid: He Stole Sheep

John Reid's story is pretty typical of the time. Though he was not a very bad man, his exploits were to cost him very dearly.

He was born in 1725 in Muiravonside, Stirlingshire. His dad was a butcher but John grew up with little money and few prospects for the future. He was working on sheep farms by the age of eight, and then he trained to be a butcher like his father. He finally settled down with a wife, living at Hillend, near Avonbridge.

It all started to go wrong when Reid's parents died. He inherited a small amount of money but this was soon gone. He found himself on the wrong side of the law and only escaped a spell in prison by agreeing to join the army.

When Reid finally returned to Scotland in 1766, he was a ticking time-bomb. He continued to rob and steal and was finally caught taking 120 sheep. He was tried in court but was found not guilty, thanks to a brilliant lawyer (Reid even boasted that he was guilty after the trial!).

It all came to a head in 1773 when Reid was accused of stealing 19 sheep from a farm in nearby Peeblesshire. It is probable that Reid didn't actually steal the sheep but had bought them from a shady character, knowing full well that they had been stolen, which was also a crime. The fact that Reid tried to run away to England – he was caught – didn't help his case. He was put on trial. Reid once again called on his brilliant lawyer, but this time he was found guilty and sentenced to death.

Many people believed that the death sentence was being used too much and that it was wrong to sentence a man to be hanged for stealing sheep. Reid's lawyer campaigned for him not to be killed, but with no luck. On 21 September 1774, Reid was hanged at the Grassmarket in Edinburgh. His lifeless body hung at the end of the rope, swinging gently in the breeze for over an hour before it was finally cut down and buried at Muiravonside.

James Aitken:

A Thief with a Burning Desire

It all started so well for James Aitken. By 1774 he had grown up in Edinburgh, attended university and trained to be a painter. Unlike most young men at the time he had the world at his feet. However, things started to go wrong when he moved to London. He tried his hand at burgling houses, robbing a few people on the street and even had a go at being a highwayman. By 1775 the police were on his tail and he ran away to America.

At the time, America was ruled by the English, but a growing number of American rebels wanted them out. Aitken got to know these men. He returned to England a year later, ready to help his new friends get their freedom from their English leaders.

Aitken's plan was simple, if a bit stupid. He would burn down the English dockyards in Portsmouth. This was where many ships docked and unloaded their goods. Aitken designed a special device for starting the fires, but there were two problems. First, he had no money. Second, he had no one to make the devices. To solve the first problem he set out to Paris and met with American rebel Silas Deane. Deane was not convinced by Aitken's plan (which, after all, was a bit stupid), but was happy to give the man some cash. With his money Aitken returned to England and paid a tinsmith in Canterbury to make his devices. It was all going well . . .

Aitken moved to Portsmouth and managed to get himself a job at the docks. One night he set up one of his devices in a rope house. Unfortunately, it failed to go off, so Aitken started a fire nearby and did a runner. The rope house caught alight, but the fire was soon put out and the rope house rebuilt. Aitken moved to Plymouth and then Bristol. In Bristol he set alight a string of fires in the dockyards. These fires did some damage but nothing like the fiery inferno he had dreamed of starting.

In December 1776 the police released a description of the man they wanted to arrest for burning down the rope house in Portsmouth.

The man was called John the Painter, 'was twenty-five or twenty-six years old, thin, 5 feet 7 inches tall, with a fair complexion and sandy hair, last seen wearing a faded brown surtout coat and cocked hat'. Aitken was quickly caught, not by the police but by two men whose houses he had robbed years before.

Now, you may have already guessed this, but Aitken was not the brightest of men. When he was arrested he kept his mouth shut and said nothing. The police had no evidence. He might well have gone free. However, while they looked for evidence Aitken was thrown into prison and it was here that Aitken started to blab, telling his cellmate everything he had been up to in the last few years. The cellmate told the police and James Aitken was put on trial.

We have seen from John Reid that you can get away with just about anything, stealing sheep in his case, if you have a good lawyer. Aitken decided to sack his lawyer and instead defend himself. Big mistake. In the end, 20 people turned up in court to say they had seen Aitken committing crimes. Do you know how many Aitken was able to find to say he was innocent? None. Not one person would stand up in court and say John Aitken had not committed a crime.

The judge had little choice but to find Aitken guilty and sentence him to be hanged. Aitken was finally executed on Portsmouth Common. He was hanged from the mast of a ship called the *Arethusa*, which had been erected in the common just for him. His body was left hanging for years and people took to stealing bits from his decaying body! To this day Portsmouth City Museum owns a mummified finger which is said to have belonged to John the Painter.

David Haggart: The Man in the Iron Mask

Our next thief is a slippery character who would not stay caught. David Haggart was born at Goldenacre, Canonmills, Edinburgh, on 24 June 1801. His father was a gamekeeper and the boy received a good education. Yet Haggart is recorded saying that it was 'his fate' to become criminal and as a teenager he had already become a pickpocket.

In 1813 he made one final attempt to avoid a life of crime and joined the army as a drummer boy. He was sent back to Edinburgh but the big crowds and easy pickings were just too much of a temptation and Haggart was soon picking pockets once again.

Haggart was restless and travelled across the country in search of prey. He would visit fairs in Kendal, Carlisle, Newcastle, and sometimes as far north as Aberdeen. His luck finally ran out in 1818. Having moved up from simple pickpocketing to breaking into houses, he was caught burgling a house in Durham. The judge sent Haggart to prison.

Our hero was far from the ideal prisoner and really didn't like being locked up. In fact, he made it his business to escape whenever possible. Over the next few years he

was sent to prison six times. On four occasions he broke out of the prison and escaped. It was on the last of these break-outs that it all went very badly wrong.

On 10 October 1820, when escaping from Dumfries Tolbooth, Haggart smacked one of the guards, Thomas Morring, with a stone and killed him. Haggart fled to Ireland. However, he was recognised in Belfast and arrested. Slippery Haggart promptly escaped only to be re-rearrested in Dublin. This time the police were taking no risks. They wrapped him in chains and placed a large, heavy, iron mask on his head. Haggart was transported to Edinburgh to face trail. He was found guilty. On 18 July 1821 a large crowd gathered to watch David Haggart hanged. This was one fate from which he couldn't escape!

Johnny Ramensky: A Cracking Criminal

Does doing bad things make you a bad person? If you are a good guy all your life, you know saving kittens from trees and helping grannies across the road, but then decide to rob sweets from the local newsagent, does this make you a bad person?

Here's the story of Johnny Ramensky. Read it through and decide if a bad guy can also be a good guy . . .

Jonas Ramanauckas was born in 1905. His dad was Lithuanian and the family lived in a mining village in North Lanarkshire. No one is quite sure when Jonas changed his name to Johnny, but that's what we will call him. The young boy's life was hard – he helped his father down the mines. His father's job was to use dynamite to blow up the rock and expose the coal.

You be careful with that dynamite.

After the First World War, Johnny and his family moved to Glasgow. They had little money and were forced to live in a slum area known as the Gorbals. Johnny's days down the mines had taught him to be tough and agile, ideal skills for his next career move – burglary!

Johnny Ramensky refused to rob people's houses and instead focused on businesses he knew were empty at the time. His trademark break-in was to climb up the pipes on the outside of the building and then force his way in through an open window. Johnny soon learned how to pick locks and eventually became an expert at opening safes. Despite Johnny's speed and strength, he never resorted to violence, earning himself the nickname of 'Gentle Johnny'.

He was first caught by the police when he was 18 years old and was to spend the rest of his life in and out of prison. In fact, he ended up spending more years behind bars than he did on the streets. In 1934, whilst in prison yet again, he heard that his young wife had died. The prison wardens refused to let him leave prison to go to the funeral, so Johnny decided to escape. It turned out he was as good at getting out of prisons as he was at breaking into buildings!

A few years after Johnny was recaptured, the Second World War broke out. The British army decided that a man with Johnny's skills would be useful so they offered him a pardon if he joined the Commandos. This meant that after he fought in the war, he would be free.

Johnny jumped at the chance. It was decided that the best way to use Johnny was to parachute him behind enemy lines to crack open their safes and steal secrets. Johnny Ramensky was dropped into North Africa and

Germany, and later joined the attack on Italy. As the war drew to a close, Johnny was one of the first soldiers to enter Rome. In the space of one day he cracked 14 safes!

When the war was over, Johnny returned to Glasgow a free man. Can you guess what he was doing within a couple of months? Breaking and entering. The excitement of the war was over and so Johnny returned to what he knew best – robbing and being caught.

In 1955 he was sentenced to 10 years 'preventive detention' in prison. This meant that, although he would be behind bars, he would have more freedom than most prisoners, with many treats and goodies. However, after two years none of these treats and goodies had appeared. So Johnny did what he did best – he escaped. Johnny was soon recaptured and returned to Peterhead Prison. This was considered one of the strongest and most secure prisons in Scotland. In 1958, Johnny Ramensky made a mockery of prison security, escaping a total of five times.

Johnny was never able to stay out of prison and in 1972 he collapsed and died in Perth Prison. His funeral was well attended, with cops and criminals standing side-by-side to say goodbye to a well-loved Scottish criminal and war hero.

Burke and Hare: Body-snatchers

We can't leave our sordid survey of Scottish criminals without a final visit to Victorian Edinburgh and a quick glimpse into the world of the body-snatcher. Our final story begins in Edinburgh in the nineteenth century with a doctor called Robert Knox. He was a lecturer at Edinburgh University, teaching young doctors all about anatomy. This is the study of the human body. The best way for doctors to learn about how the body works is to cut up a real body and delve into all that muscle, skin and bones.

Knox got his bodies from the courts – you see, the only dead bodies that were allowed to be cut up were those of criminals that had been executed. Now, you might think after reading this book that a lot of people were executed in Edinburgh, but that wasn't really the case. Executions were actually pretty rare and this meant that Knox quickly ran out of bodies to cut up.

Knox had a solution to the problem of not having enough bodies – he paid people for corpses. If you turned up at Knox's house, dead body in tow, he would pay you for the body – *no questions asked*. This led to lots of bodies being stolen and given to Knox. The problem became so bad that when a person died, relatives would stand over the body until it was buried and then guard the grave until the rot had set in and the bodies were useless to Knox.

Body-snatching dead bodies is one thing, but two men called Burke and Hare came up with a better idea . . .

Burke and Hare

Brendan Burke and William Hare were both Irish workmen who moved to Edinburgh to help build canals. In late 1827, Burke moved into a guesthouse at Tanner's Close, in the West Port area of Edinburgh, which was owned by Hare and his wife. It was here that the two men became close friends. Their body-snatching antics began soon afterwards.

An old soldier, who had also been lodging in Hare's guesthouse, died of natural causes. Burke and Hare offered to remove the body, but instead of having it buried they filled a coffin with old bark and buried that instead. They then took the soldier's body to Knox who was happy to pay them for their trouble.

Burke and Hare realised they were on to a nice little earner. If only they could somehow have access to more dead bodies . . .

They struck luck when fellow lodger Joseph the Miller fell ill. His was not a fatal illness until Burke and Hare got involved. The pair gave Joseph lots of whisky and when he was very drunk they suffocated the poor fellow. Once dead, they took the body to Knox and collected their cash.

So far so good

In February 1828 Burke and Hare invited pensioner Abigail Simpson to spend the night in the guesthouse. Once she was safely in her room, the pair went to her with a bottle of whisky, got her drunk, and suffocated her just as they had done to Joseph the Miller. Once again, they took the body through the streets of Edinburgh to Knox, who was happy to pay them for new meat – *no questions asked*.

Next on the list were Mary Patterson and Janet Brown. Burke met the two women in Canongate and invited them to breakfast at the guesthouse. When they arrived the next morning there seemed to be a strange tension in the air. The breakfast was strained and an argument soon broke out. Janet Brown stormed out but returned a few hours later. She arrived to find that Mary Patterson was nowhere to been seen. She was told that she had left. Mary Patterson, in fact, turned up next day on Knox's dissecting table. It is rumoured that some of Knox's students actually recognised the dead body.

They just keep coming

Burke and Hare were becoming good at killing and were greedy for the money – a dangerous combination. The next victim was a beggar called Effie, who Burke befriended, rescued, killed and delivered to Knox. Burke was busy again soon afterwards. He saw a woman being arrested by the police, but saved her by saying he knew her and would look after her. She was murdered and delivered to Knox a few hours later.

And they didn't stop.

The next two victims were a grandmother and her blind grandson. The old lady was killed with a dose of painkillers. The blind grandson met a far more painful end with Hare stretching the boy across his knee and breaking his back. Knox was grateful for two more bodies, *no questions asked*. Mrs Ostler and Ann Dougal followed shortly after, with Knox again taking the bodies. Elizabeth Haldane was killed after taking refuge in Hare's stable. Her daughter was killed and delivered to Knox a few months later. Knox never once asked where the bodies were coming from.

The pair's next victim did start to raise some questions, but not from Knox. Burke and Hare picked on a well-known local boy, just 18 years old, nicknamed 'Daft Jamie'. After the body was delivered to Knox, his students recognised the dead body and asked if it was Daft Jamie. Knox said it was not, but started the dissection face first so that no more questions could be asked. Knox didn't like questions!

Burke and Hare's final victim was Marjory Campbell Docherty. She was lured into Hare's guest house. There were two lodgers already staying at the house so Hare had to wait until James and Ann Gray had gone out for the night before killing Marjory. The next morning neighbours complained they had heard a struggle the night before. Ann Gray also became suspicious when Hare refused to let her back into her old room to collect some clothes she had forgotten to pack. The Grays waited until Hare left the building and went back to their room. They found the body of Marjory Campbell Docherty under the bed.

The police were called but Burke and Hare had removed
the body before they arrived. However, the police received

a tip-off from one of Knox's students. When the police
went to the university they found the body of Marjory
Campbell Docherty on the dissecting table and arrested
Burke and Hare.

Despite almost a year of killing, the police couldn't find
much evidence of the murders. After all, the bodies had
been sliced and diced by Knox and his students. In the end
it was Hare that ensured Burke's downfall. The police told
Hare that if he gave evidence against Burke then he would
go free. Hare jumped at the chance. He spilled the beans,
giving full details of the killing.

On 28 January 1829 Burke was hanged. His body was then taken down and delivered to Edinburgh University. Alexander Monro, the professor in charge, proceeded to dissect the murderer's body. He is said to have dipped his quill pen into Burke's blood and written, 'This is written with the blood of Wm Burke, who was hanged at Edinburgh. This blood was taken from his head.'

And what became of William Hare? He was released a few months later. Some say he became a blind beggar on the streets of London. Others say he was recognised and killed by an angry mob. The last mark that Hare made on history was a sighting in the town of Carlisle, and then he disappeared forever.